W9-BMU-616

Please return to
the ESL room,
Karen Gibson

The *Chinese Americans*

SENIOR CONSULTING EDITOR

SENATOR DANIEL PATRICK MOYNIHAN

CONSULTING EDITORS

ANN ORLOV
Managing Editor, Harvard
Encyclopedia of American
Ethnic Groups

M. MARK STOLARIK
President, The Balch Institute for
Ethnic Studies, Philadelphia

DAVID M. REIMERS
Professor of History, New York
University

JAMES F. WATTS
Chairman, History Department,
City College of New York

The Chinese Americans

William Daley

Sandra Stotsky, General Editor
Harvard University Graduate School of Education

CHELSEA HOUSE PUBLISHERS

New York • Philadelphia

CHELSEA HOUSE PUBLISHERS

Editorial Director: Richard Rennert
Executive Managing Editor: Karyn Gullen Browne
Copy Chief: Robin James
Picture Editor: Adrian G. Allen
Creative Director: Robert Mitchell
Art Director: Joan Ferrigno
Production Manager: Sallye Scott

THE IMMIGRANT EXPERIENCE

Editors: Rebecca Stefoff and Reed Ueda

Staff for THE CHINESE AMERICANS

Assistant Editor: Annie McDonnell
Copy Editor: Apple Kover
Assistant Designer: Lydia Rivera
Cover Illustrator: Jane Sterrett

Copyright © 1996 by Chelsea House Publishers, a division of Main Line Book Co. All rights reserved. Printed and bound in the United States of America.

3 5 7 9 8 6 4 2

Daley, William.
   The Chinese Americans / William Daley.
   p. cm.—(The immigrant experience)
   Includes bibliographical references (p.) and index.
   ISBN 0-7910-3357-0.
        0-7910-3379-1 (pbk.)
   1. Chinese Americans—Juvenile literature. [1. Chinese Americans.] I. Title. II. Series.
E184.C5D35   1996   94-45788
973′.04951—dc20   CIP
                                                                              AC

CONTENTS

THE IMMIGRANT EXPERIENCE

CHELSEA HOUSE PUBLISHERS

A NATION OF NATIONS

Senator Daniel Patrick Moynihan

The Constitution of the United States begins: "We the People of the United States . . ." Yet, as we know, the United States is not made up of a single group of people. It is made up of many peoples. Immigrants from Europe, Asia, Africa, South America, and Australia settled in North America seeking a new life filled with opportunities unavailable in their homeland. Coming from many nations, they forged one nation and made it their own. More than 100 years ago, Walt Whitman expressed this perception of America as a melting pot: "Here is not merely a nation, but a teeming Nation of nations."

It was the ingenuity and acts of courage of these immigrants, our ancestors, that shaped the North American way of life. Yet, we sometimes take their contributions for granted. This fine series, *The Peoples of North America*, examines the experiences and contributions of the immigrants and how these contributions determined the future of the United States, Canada, and Mexico.

The immigrants did not abandon their ethnic traditions when they reached the shores of North America. Each ethnic group had its own customs and traditions, and each brought different experiences, accomplishments, skills, values, styles of dress, and tastes in food that lingered long after its arrival. Yet this profusion of differences created a singularity, or bond, among the immigrants. The poet Robert Frost put it well: "The land was ours before we were the land's."

The United States and Canada are unique in this respect. Whereas religious and ethnic differences sparked wars throughout the rest of the world—from the 17th-century religious wars to the 19th-century nationalist movements in Europe to the near extermination of the Jews under Nazi Germany—*we* learned to respect each other's differences and to live as one.

And the differences were as varied as the millions of immigrants who sought a new life in North America. In a mass migration, some 12 million immigrants passed through the waiting rooms of New York's Ellis Island; thousands more came to the West Coast. At first, these immigrants were welcomed because labor was needed to meet the demands of the Industrial Age. Soon, however, the new immigrants faced the prejudice of earlier immigrants who saw them as a burden on the economy. Legislation was passed to limit immigration. The Chinese Exclusion Act of 1882 was among the first laws closing the doors to the promise of America. The Japanese were also effectively excluded by this law. In 1924, Congress established immigration quotas on a country-by-country basis.

Such prejudices might have erupted into war, as they did in Europe, but North Americans chose negotiation and compromise, instead. This determination to resolve differences peacefully has been the hallmark of the countries of North America.

The unique ability of Americans to live together as one people was seriously threatened by the issue of slavery. It was a symptom of a growing attitude of intolerance in the world. Thousands of English settlers had arrived in the colonies as indentured servants. These Englishmen agreed to work for a specified number of years on a farm or as a craftsman's apprentice in return for passage to America and room and board. When the first Africans arrived in the then-British colonies during the 17th century, some colonists thought that they should be treated as indentured servants, too. Eventually, the question of whether the Africans should be considered indentured, like the Englishmen, or slaves who could be owned for life, was considered in a Maryland court. The court's calamitous decree held that blacks were slaves bound to lifelong servitude, and so were their children. America went through a time of moral examination and civil war pitting brother against brother before it finally freed African slaves, as well as their descendants. The principle that all men are created equal had faced its greatest challenge and survived.

The court ruling that set blacks apart from other races fanned flames of discrimination that lasted long after slavery was abolished. The concept of racism had existed for centuries in countries throughout the world. When the Manchus conquered China in the 17th century, they decreed that Chinese and Manchus could not intermarry. To impress their superiority on the conquered Chinese, the Manchus ordered all Chinese men to wear their hair in a long braid called a queue.

By the 19th century, some intellectuals took up the banner of racism, citing Charles Darwin's work on the evolution of animals as proof of their position. Darwin's studies theorized that highly evolved animals were dominant over other animals. Some advocates of this theory applied it to humans, asserting that certain races were more highly evolved than others and thus were superior.

This philosophy served as the basis for a new discrimination, not only against certain races, but also against various ethnic groups. These ugly ideas were directed at black people and other victims as well. Asians faced harsh discrimination and were depicted by 19th-century newspaper cartoonists who chronicled public opinion as depraved, degenerate people, deficient in intelligence. When the Irish flooded American cities to escape the famine in

Ireland, the cartoonists caricatured the typical "Paddy" (a popular term for Irish immigrants) as an apelike creature with jutting jaw and sloping forehead.

By the 20th century, these concepts of racism and ethnic prejudice had developed into virulent theories of a Northern European master race. When Adolf Hitler came to power in Germany in 1933, he popularized the notion of Aryan supremacy. "Aryan," a term referring to the Indo-European races, was applied to so-called superior physical characteristics such as blond hair, blue eyes, and delicate facial features. Anyone with darker and heavier features was considered inferior. Buttressed by these theories, the German Nazi state from 1933 to 1945 set out to destroy European Jews, along with Gypsies and other groups considered inferior. It nearly succeeded. Millions of these people were killed.

How supremely important it is, then, that we have learned to live with one another, respecting differences while treasuring the things we share.

A relatively recent example of this nonviolent way of resolving differences is the solution the Canadians found to a conflict between two ethnic groups. The conflict arose in the mid-1960s between the peoples of French-speaking Quebec Province and those of the English-speaking provinces. Relations grew tense, then bitter, then violent. The Royal Commission on Bilingualism and Biculturalism was established to study the growing crisis and to propose measures to ease the tensions. As a result of the commission's recommendations, all official documents and statements from the national government's capital at Ottawa are now issued in both French and English, and bilingual education is encouraged.

The year 1980 marked a coming of age for the United States' ethnic heritage. For the first time, the U.S. Census asked people about their ethnic background. Americans chose from more than 100 groups, including French Basque, Spanish Basque, French Canadian, Afro-American, Peruvian, Armenian, Chinese, and Japanese, among others. The ethnic group with the largest response was English (49.6 million). More than 100 million Americans claimed ancestors from the British Isles, which includes Ireland, Wales, and Scotland. There were almost as many Germans (49.2 million) as English. The Irish-American population (40.2 million) was third, but the next largest ethnic group, the Afro-Americans, was a distant fourth (21 million). There was a sizable group of French ancestry (13 million), as well as of Italian (12 million). Poles, Dutch, Swedes, Norwegians, and Russians followed. These groups, and other smaller ones, represent the wondrous profusion of ethnic influences in North America.

Canada, too, has discovered the diversity of its population. Studies conducted during the French/English conflict determined that Canadians were descended from Ukrainians, Germans, Italians, Chinese, Japanese, native Indians, and Eskimos. Canada found it had no ethnic majority, although nearly half of its immigrant population came from the British Isles. Canada, like the United States, is a land of immigrants for whom mutual tolerance is a matter of reason as well as principle. Tolerance is a virtue that has brought North America peace.

The people of North America are the descendants of one of the greatest migrations in history. That migration is not over. Koreans, Vietnamese, Nicaraguans, and Cubans are heading for the shores of North America in large numbers. This mix of cultures shapes every aspect of our lives. To understand ourselves, we must know something about our ethnic ancestry, as well as about the ancestry of others, because in a sense, they are part of our history, too. Nothing so defines the North American nations as the motto on the Great Seal of the United States: *E Pluribus Unum*—Out of Many, One.

FROM CHINA TO AMERICA

In 1990, the U.S. census showed that 0.7 percent of the country's population was of Chinese descent. More than 1,645,000 people living in the United States now identify themselves as being of Chinese origin. Some of these people are the descendants of men and women who came to America from China generations earlier. Others are recent arrivals in the United States from China or from the islands of Hong Kong and Taiwan, which lie off the coast of China and are populated by people who are ethnically Chinese. There are enormous differences among the Chinese in America. Some, the third- and fourth-generation children of immigrants, speak no Chinese and have little or no connection with their ancestors' homeland. Among the recent arrivals are many who do not yet speak English and retain strong family ties to the old country. Some Chinese Americans are prosperous; others are struggling to make ends meet. Together they form a dynamic, varied, and fast-growing segment of the U.S. population.

13

■ *A late-19th-century magazine illustration shows immigrant laundry workers.*

People from China began coming to the United States in the mid-19th century. The majority of the early Chinese immigrants were men. Few Chinese women immigrated until the middle of the 20th century. One reason for this was that during much of the history of Chinese immigration, the government of China permitted people to leave the country only if work awaited them, and in the 19th and early 20th centuries, most jobs were reserved for men. But the women stayed in China for other reasons as well. One of the most important reasons was that

14

many of the men who emigrated from China to the United States, leaving their families behind, did not expect to be away for more than a few years. Those who had wives expected to be reunited with them, and those who were not married planned to return to China to marry. Women were also kept from emigrating by tradition, which held women responsible for the care of their husbands' parents. It is likely that more Chinese women would have come to the United States if not for a series of American laws which, beginning in 1882, severely restricted Chinese immigration, making it difficult for men as well as women to gain entrance to the United States.

In the end, many of the men who had come to America in the first wave of immigration did not return to China. They lived out their lives in the United States, but the shortage of Chinese women in America,

A child, rare among the early settlers, was especially cherished.

15

 *Chinatowns are still a starting point for many immigrants.*

together with laws in some places that prevented marriages between Chinese and non-Chinese people, meant that most of these men were unable to marry and raise families. The Chinese community in America was largely one of bachelors until the middle of the 20th century, when changes in both Chinese and American laws meant that Chinese immigrants could begin coming to the United States as families. The Chinese are still coming, and now women outnumber men among new immigrants from China—52 percent of all Chinese immigrants are women. This second wave of immigration from China has made the Chinese the third largest group of immigrants in the United States, after Mexicans and Filipinos.

Celia Chiang is an example of the new Chinese immigrant. Her story shows the success that many Chinese have found in America. In the 1930s, Chiang was one of 13 children of a prominent government official in Beijing, the capital of China. When occupying Japanese forces confiscated her family's property during World War II (1939–45), Chiang walked nearly 1,000 miles from Beijing to the city of

Chonqqing, which was in a part of China not occupied by Japan. When the war ended, Chiang moved to the southern port city of Shanghai, but that city soon fell to the Chinese Communists, who were struggling for control of China. To escape the strife and the uncertain future offered by Communism, Chiang packed her bags again. Eventually, in 1958, she made her way to San Francisco, where one of her sisters was living. Chiang went into business in California, and by the age of 65 she owned four successful Chinese restaurants there. She is just one of many immigrants who have contributed to the diversity of the Chinese-American population.

2

EMIGRATION OFFERS HOPE

Europeans began trading with China in the 17th century, although they were allowed to enter only two port cities because China's rulers were determined to keep contact between their country and the rest of the world to a carefully controlled minimum. In 1757, foreign trade was restricted to a single port, Canton (now called Guangzhou), on the southern coast. For nearly a century, European ideas and products could enter China only through Guangzhou.

19

Trade between the United States and China began in 1784, when the American ship *Empress of China* sailed up the Pearl River into Guangzhou. The Americans on the ship stared in wide-eyed wonder at the Chinese junks, barges, and flower boats on the river. They exchanged their cargo for Chinese teas, porcelains, silks, carpets, spices, and other products that soon made their way into the most fashionable American homes. An attractive profit from their sale in the United States encouraged American merchants to enter the China trade, but for many years the United States's political involvement in China was far less than that of the European nations, particularly Great Britain.

Floating homes were one element of a culture that Americans found exotic.

■ *Tea-pickers, such as those pictured above, supplied Britain's growing demand for the leaves that produced the country's most popular beverage.*

In the 19th century, the Western nations entered the age of the Industrial Revolution, a period of technological development that saw the growth of factories and mass-produced goods. As they became increasingly industrialized, Great Britain and other European nations needed new international markets for the goods they produced. China showed little interest in these goods, however, and resisted European pressure for increased trade. Portuguese and British traders undermined China's resistance by introducing the addictive drug opium to China. Demand for opium grew quickly, and British opium plantations in India flourished as they met the demand. Recognizing the damage that the drug was doing to the Chinese people and economy, China's rulers tried to ban its sale. But corrupt Chinese port officials and smugglers, reluctant to give up their enormous profits, conspired with foreign traders to keep the trade alive.

In the mid-19th century, China and Britain twice went to war over the opium trade, with China insisting on its right to keep foreign traders

21

out of the country and the Europeans asserting their right to trade freely. England, with its powerful navy, defeated the Chinese in the first Opium War (1839–42) and forced China to open four other ports to foreign trade. The Treaty of Nanking, which ended the war, also granted Britain control of Hong Kong. Not satisfied with these concessions, the British instigated the second Opium War (1856–60) and demanded that the Chinese government sign the Treaty of Tientsin. This treaty granted Western powers the use of two more Chinese ports,

■ *Bamboo-furniture manufacturers provided a popular Chinese export.*

■ **These Chinese war junks were no match for the British naval fleet.**

23

greater freedom of movement throughout the country, and an increase in Christian missionary activity within China. The subsequent flood of mass-produced European goods, such as cloth and pottery, brought about the end of many traditional Chinese handicraft industries. Foreign trade thus enriched foreigners and Chinese officials but did little to improve the lives of the typical peasant family. For many Chinese, life became harder than ever during the 19th century.

A Life of Hardship

Traditionally, Chinese society was rigidly divided into three classes. At the bottom was the largest segment of the population, the peasant class; most of China's large population belonged to this group. Peasants were farmers, fisherfolk, or humble artisans. They lived in rural villages, rented small plots of land to farm (very few owned their own property), and generally struggled to make ends meet, to pay their landlords, and to pay the ever-increasing taxes that kept the empire going. Above them was a much smaller class that consisted of wealthy merchants and landowners as well as scholars and government officials. The topmost and smallest class consisted of China's imperial dynasty, or ruling family. Since 1644, China had been ruled by the Qing dynasty, sometimes called the Manchu dynasty (the Manchus were originally invaders from Manchuria, a region northeast of Beijing that is now part of China).

The 18th and 19th centuries saw a rapid rise in China's population, which grew from 150 million in 1700 to 400 million in 1850. Because the population grew so fast, the country's farmers were not always able to produce enough food. To make matters worse, in many years various parts of the country were struck by floods or droughts, severely reducing the wheat and rice harvests. Famine struck some regions again and again. Guangdong province, on the south coast, was one of the most populous parts of China—and also one of the hardest hit by food shortages. In the middle years of the 19th century, Guangdong also suffered from massive floods, from bloody ethnic strife between rival groups fighting for control of the fertile farmlands in the Pearl River delta, and from the effects of the two British opium wars. Many people in the region hovered near starvation. One man from Guangdong later described his family's circumstances:

> There were four in our family, my mother, my father, my sister and me. We lived in a two-room house. Our sleeping room and the other served as parlor, kitchen, and dining room. We were not rich enough to keep pigs or fowls, otherwise, our small house would have been more than overcrowded.
>
> How can we live on six baskets of rice which were paid twice a year for my father's duty as night watchman? Sometimes the peasants have a poor crop and then we go hungry. . . . Sometimes we went hungry for days. My mother and me would go over the harvested rice fields of the peasants to pick the grains they had dropped. . . . We had only salt and water to eat with the rice.

The grim conditions under which most Chinese peasants lived offered little hope for the future. Yet the suffering of the humble Chinese occasionally erupted into widespread peasant rebellions. The most dramatic of these was the Taiping Rebellion (1850-1864). Hoping to overthrow the hated Manchu rulers, the Taiping rebels roused hundreds of thousands of peasants to battle. They quickly seized control of southeastern China, but then the rebellion lost momentum as its leaders fell to quarreling among themselves. Eventually the rebellion was crushed by imperial forces, but the once-productive southeastern provinces had been devastated by war and as many as 20 million people had been killed.

Rebellion was not the only outlet for China's desperate peasants. Some of them sought to improve their circumstances by emigrating, or leaving, their homeland. For many years imperial laws had forbidden Chinese people to leave China, but nonetheless the Chinese had long been emigrating to other countries. By the mid-19th century, there were Chinese communities in India, the Philippines, Malaysia, Southeast Asia, Indonesia, and even the east coast of Africa. In the second half of the 19th century, the Chinese government loosened its ban on emigration, allowing Chinese people to go abroad to work. Between

1850 and 1900, more than 2 million Chinese—less than half of 1 percent of the country's total population—left their homeland. Some went to neighboring Asian countries and islands. Others ventured farther, to North and South America and the Caribbean. Most of the emigrants from China came from the southeastern provinces of Guangdong and Fujian, and nearly all of those who came to North America during this period were from a small region within Guangdong.

Fragrant Hills and Gold Mountains

As early as the 18th century, a few Chinese sailors and laborers had ventured to the Polynesian kingdom of Hawaii, where they harvested the sweet-scented timber of the sandalwood tree, which was greatly prized in China. The sandalwood gave Hawaii its Chinese nickname, Tan Heung Shan, which means "Fragrant Sandalwood Hills." The sandalwood had been harvested right out of existence in Hawaii by the mid-19th century, but by that time American investors had begun operating sugarcane plantations there, and Chinese immigrants were imported to work on these plantations. About 46,000 Chinese went to Hawaii in the second half of the 19th century.

Another destination also beckoned to the Chinese emigrants. This destination was farther away, clear across the ocean: California, where gold had been discovered in 1848. Rumors of the gold strike reached Guangdong province, spreading gold fever among the Chinese. One young man in Guangzhou wrote, "Good many Americans speak of California. Oh! Very rich country! I hear good many Americans and Europeans go there. Oh! They find gold very quickly, so I hear." The first big wave of gold miners to reach California—called the forty-niners because they arrived in 1849—included 325 Chinese men who dreamed of making their fortunes in Gold Mountain. By the 1850s, gold fever had lured more than 20,000 Chinese to San Francisco.

Even without the lure of gold, California was attractive to poor Chinese who were desperate for work. During the 1860s, for example, a

Chinese laborer who might earn the equivalent of $3 to $5 a month in Guangdong province could earn as much as $30 a month in the United States. Drawn by the promise of good wages, emigrants shipped out to the West Coast of North America in ever-growing numbers. In all, some 380,000 Chinese entered the United States mainland between 1849 and 1930. They were the first wave of Chinese immigrants in America, the foundation of today's Chinese-American community.

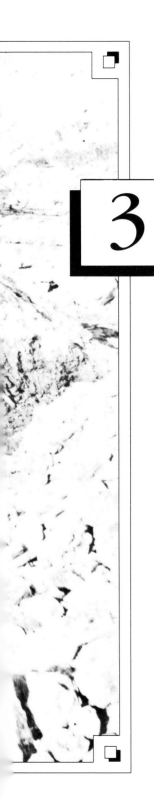

3

T HE
FIRST WAVE

The great majority of the Chinese in the first wave of immigration were men. As a result, Chinese men far outnumbered Chinese women in the United States. By 1900, there were almost 90,000 Chinese people on the U.S. mainland, but only 5 percent of them were women.

These Chinese immigrants did not plan to settle permanently in North America or Hawaii. They intended to work for a few years, save money, and then return home to China in triumph. Many of them had left wives and families at home. Most were peasants with little or no education, although the first wave of immigration also included some merchants and artisans who sensed new business opportunities outside their homeland.

Some of the more prosperous emigrants could pay for their passage to Hawaii or North America, but most emigrants could not afford to buy steamship tickets. There were two ways for them to go abroad. They could go as contract workers, which meant that they agreed to work for a specific number of years for a particular employer, who then paid for their passage. Or they could travel under the credit-ticket system, in which their employer—or a middleman called a broker—paid for their passage; the emigrant agreed to repay the cost of the ticket from his future earnings. (Americans sometimes mistakenly called all Chinese immigrants "coolies," but the coolie system, in which laborers were tricked or forced into a type of slave labor, was not used in Hawaii or the United States, although some Chinese laborers in Cuba and South America were coolies.)

For most of the immigrants, the passage across the Pacific Ocean, whether to Hawaii or to the West Coast of North America, was a miserable experience. They traveled on the least costly tickets, which meant that they were steerage passengers, crammed into overcrowded, stifling compartments below decks. Their food was of poor quality, they had no facilities for washing, and disease was rampant. In addition, many passengers, unaccustomed to ocean travel, were desperately seasick. One Chinese immigrant wrote, "I ate wind and tasted water for more than twenty days."

■ *Chinese miners often worked claims others had abandoned.*

◳ *Illustrations of the day glamorized worker accommodations.*

Working in America

Many of the Chinese who came to America in the 1850s went to the gold fields, hoping to win their fortunes. They soon became known for their hard work, their ingenuity, and their success at finding gold—not always in great quantities, but gold nevertheless—on claims that other miners had given up as worthless. The Chinese miners worked diligently and introduced techniques and equipment that had been developed in the mines of China over the years. Another key to the success of the Chinese, in mining and in other ventures as well, was that they worked together cooperatively and pooled their resources. For example, often a group of men, perhaps relatives or emigrants from the same village in China, would join together to purchase a mining claim, work together to extract the gold, and then share in the profits.

By the mid-1860s, the gold fields were becoming played out. Small individual claims held little remaining gold; only the large corporate mining operations, which used expensive machinery, continued to pro-

duce significant amounts of ore. The Chinese immigrants began look-ing for other work. Many of them turned to the railroad companies that were busy laying track across the American West. The Central Pacific Railroad, charged with building a railway eastward from the California Coast across the rugged and forbidding Sierra Nevada range and the desolate Great Basin of Nevada, hired its first Chinese laborers in 1865. Two years later, 90 percent of the company's workforce was Chinese. Supervisors were delighted with the skill and reliability of the Chinese

By the 1850s, Chinese miners were a familiar sight in the gold fields of California. They also mined gold, silver, and coal in Nevada, Idaho, Colorado, Montana, Alaska, and British Columbia.

workers, who performed all sorts of tasks from clearing forests to building bridges to blasting tunnels through mountains with dynamite.

The railroad company was also pleased that the Chinese workers were more economical to employ than white workers. The Chinese agreed to pay for their food and lodging in the work camps out of their wages; white workers demanded that their food and lodging be provided by the company. In addition, the Chinese workers, who did not have a tradition of organized labor activity, were less likely than other groups of workers to go on strike and demand higher wages. When a group of Chinese workers high in the snowbound Sierra Nevada *did* go on strike, asking for better pay and an eight-hour work day, the railroad company responded by cutting off their provisions until they returned to work.

The transcontinental railroad was completed in 1869. Some of the Chinese railroad workers went on to work on other railway lines around the country, but most of them looked for other work on the West Coast. Many found jobs in California's agricultural industry, which developed between 1860 and 1890.

Before that time, wheat was the principal crop in California. Once the California farmers began recruiting Chinese laborers, however, the Chinese demonstrated their skill in cultivating a variety of new crops: rice, vegetables, grapes, tobacco, berries, fruit trees, and flowers. The Chinese also introduced fruit-drying to the region, giving the California raisin industry its start. In addition, they used age-old Chinese techniques to drain and irrigate land, turning the Sacramento Valley from useless swamp worth only $1 to $3 per acre into valuable farmland worth $20 to $30 per acre. The Chinese helped make California into an agricultural giant, but their contributions to American agriculture reached beyond California: in Oregon, Ah Bing developed the Bing cherry, and in Florida a citrus grower named Lue Gim Gong bred the frost-resistant orange that became the foundation of Florida's citrus industry.

The early Chinese immigrants also found work on sheep and cattle ranches. In fact, the Chinese were an important part of the "Old West,"

■ *The violence directed toward Chinese laborers intensified despite their significant contributions to the development of America.*

although popular images of the West seldom reflect the presence of Chinese cowboys. Chinese workers could also be found in lumber camps and in fishing fleets and canneries from California to Alaska. Sometimes they worked as camp cooks, but they also held the same jobs as other workers.

Although Chinese people could be found throughout the United States, they were concentrated in the West, where the ports by which they entered the country were located. In 1870, more than three-fourths of all the Chinese in the country were in California, but they soon began spreading out—by 1900, only half of all Chinese lived in

California. At the same time, the Chinese were moving from the countryside to the cities. At first they were largely rural, living in work camps of one sort or another. But by the end of the 19th century, they had formed urban communities called Chinatowns in San Francisco, Sacramento, Los Angeles, Boston, New York City, and elsewhere.

The Rise of Anti-Chinese Feeling

At first the Chinese immigrants were welcomed in California and elsewhere. Before long, though, they were scorned by some other workers, who resented the fact that the Chinese were willing to work hard for low wages. Some non-Chinese people, both American-born citizens and recent immigrants from Europe, turned against the Chinese. In the California gold fields, for example, white miners sang:

> We're working like a swarm of bees scarcely making enough to live
> And two hundred thousand Chinese are taking home the gold we ought
> to have.

Part of the anti-Chinese feeling that arose in the second half of the 19th century came from some Americans' growing fear and hostility toward all foreigners, not just the Chinese. Other Asian immigrants were confronted with the same hostility and prejudice, as were many Catholic immigrants from Ireland and the southern European nations. Large sections of the United States were populated mostly—although not entirely—by white Protestants whose ancestors had come from England, Scotland, Germany, or Scandinavia. Some of these felt that they were the "true" Americans; they worried that Asian, Catholic, and Jewish immigrants would weaken America by introducing alien religions, customs, and languages. This nativism, or anti-foreigner sentiment, sometimes broke forth in expression of hostility aimed at Asians, who were easy to single out as scapegoats and were very visible, especially on the West Coast. An 1876 magazine cartoon, for example, portrayed the Statue of Liberty as she would appear if she stood in San

Francisco Bay—wearing a Chinese pigtail and haloed by the Japanese flag.

Anti-Chinese feeling did not stem from nativism alone. A large part of it was economic in origin. Other workers complained that by working for low wages, the Chinese kept everyone's wages down; some also grumbled that the immigrants were taking jobs that "belonged" to whites. These complaints increased after the United States entered a severe economic depression in 1870. The depression forced many American laborers out of work. Because the Chinese were an easily recognizable minority, they became targets for the frustration of the jobless. Tensions grew, and gangs of roughnecks attacked Chinese. In July of 1871, thousands of people attacked the Los Angeles Chinatown in a riot that lasted for three days, burning homes and businesses and robbing and killing Chinese; 19 Chinese were murdered in the riot. A simi-

A 19th-century anti-Chinese rally. An economic depression and growing nativism fueled such rallies as well as occasional outbursts of violence.

lar tragedy occurred in 1885 at Rock Springs, in the Wyoming Territory, when a group of Chinese coal miners was attacked by a mob of white miners, who killed 28 Chinese and wounded 15 more.

Although such incidents of violence were tragic, a more serious threat to the well-being of the Chinese in America came from the law

In an effort to satisfy non- Asian business owners who feared competition from Chinese workers and businesses, California passed a state law against this traditional Chinese method of carrying loads. The law was intended to make it more difficult and costly for Chinese vendors and services to operate.

and the courts. In an attempt to limit Chinese immigration, California passed laws requiring foreign miners to buy licenses and prohibiting Asian immigrants from owning land. Other states passed similar laws. Chinese Americans did not docilely submit to these conditions. When San Francisco passed a series of laws that discriminated against Chi-

nese laundries, Yick Lee, owner of the Yick Wo Laundry, took his case to court. The U.S. Supreme Court upheld *Yick* in 1886 when it ruled that the equal protection clause of the Fourteenth Amendment applied to noncitizens living in the United States. Since that time, more than 600 cases have cited the *Yick Wo* decision, which ensures equal protection for all people living in America.

"The Chinese problem"—the question of whether Chinese laborers were a source of unfair competition for other workers—was a topic of public discussion throughout the 1870s. In reality, however, the Chinese made up a tiny fraction of the American population, and the "problem" had more to do with the nation's angry and frustrated working class than with the Chinese themselves. Prejudice against the Chinese became an outlet for people's deeper concerns about unemployment, hard times, and conflict between workers and employers. Unfortunately for the Chinese, the U.S. Congress echoed this prejudice when it passed the Chinese Exclusion Act of 1882. The act barred Chinese laborers from immigrating to the United States, although Chinese merchants, teachers, students, and tourists were still permitted to enter the country. The Chinese Exclusion Act closed the door to many of the Chinese people who sought entry into the United States—for example, 40,000 Chinese had come to America in 1881, the year before the act was passed, but in 1887, five years after the passage of the act, only 10 Chinese gained entry. In 1888 Congress passed the Scott Act, which prevented Chinese who had returned to China to marry or to visit their families from re-entering the United States. As a result of these laws, the Chinese population in the United States dropped to about 60,000 in 1920.

The Chinese in Hawaii

The Chinese who went to Hawaii found themselves in a very different environment than those who went to the mainland. For one thing, there were many more Chinese women and families in Hawaii. The plantation managers encouraged their Asian workers to bring their wives and

40

(continued on page 49)

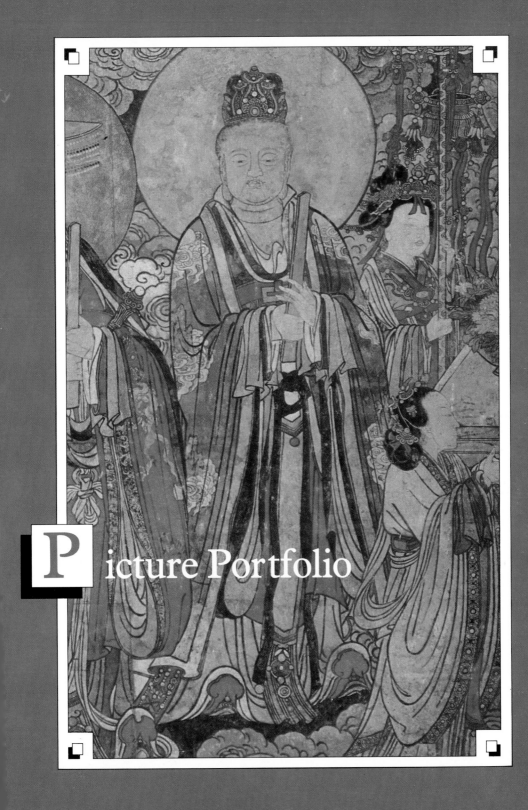

Picture Portfolio

16th-century ceramic statue of Taoist god.

Artist's depiction of entrance to Beijing's Imperial Palace.

Pagoda on Beijing's Jade Fountain Hill.

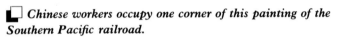 *A typical Beijing
street scene in 1926.*

*Chinese workers occupy one corner of this painting of the
Southern Pacific railroad.*

Cartoon depicts
*harassment of
immigrants.*

*An illustrat...
Chinatown para...*

*San Francisco boasts a large
Chinatown.*

■ *Colorful dragons are part of many celebrations.*

■ *Crowds gather for the New Year's parade.*

■ *Storefronts crowd New York City's Chinatown.*

■ *Window display touts ginseng's uses.*

█ *Remedies are abundant in Chinese-American herbal pharmacies.*

█ *Kuan Yin Temple in San Francisco.*

□ *A beautifully carved arch celebrates Philadelphia's Chinese-American community and invites many visitors to explore it firsthand.*

□ *New York City's Confucius Square.*

(continued from page 40)

☐ *In 1882, President Arthur limited the Exclusion Act to ten years.*

children with them because they believed that workers with families were more reliable and less likely to run away. As a result, many second-generation Chinese children were born in Hawaii in the 19th century, laying the foundations for a substantial Chinese population there.

Asians—not just Chinese but also Japanese, Koreans, and Filipinos—made up a much larger percentage of the total population in Hawaii than on the mainland. By 1920, 62 percent of Hawaii's population was Asian, compared to one-fifth of one percent of the total U.S. population. Because of this large Asian population, the Chinese in Hawaii experienced a greater degree of acceptance and toleration than many of their fellow Chinese on the mainland. Yet when the Hawaiian islands became a U.S. territory in 1898, the Chinese Exclusion Act was extended to Hawaii. The number of Chinese immigrants entering the islands fell sharply—from 5,000 in 1896 to 106 in 1906.

Some of the Chinese in Hawaii eventually returned to China, as did many of the Chinese who had entered the United States. Yet many remained, both in the islands and on the mainland. In Hawaii, the Chinese left the plantations as soon as their terms of contract labor had

□ *Because Chinese women in America were in short supply, men usually returned to China to search for wives. The Scott Act ended this practice.*

expired, opening restaurants, hotels, and other businesses in Honolulu and other cities. On the mainland, many of the immigrants who had planned to return to China after a few years had ended lived out their lives in America. Whether because they were unable to save the money for their passage home, or because their emotional ties to the homeland had weakened and they decided that they preferred life in the United States, these immigrants became permanent settlers.

4

THE GROWTH OF CHINESE AMERICA

The Chinese who came to America in search of better lives were determined to succeed. They possessed the virtues of self-reliance, patience, and diligence that remain typical of Chinese immigrants and Chinese Americans today. Alert for opportunities, many of the early immigrants went into business for themselves, serving as cooks or launderers. These were not traditional male occupations in China, but the Chinese men in the United States learned to perform them in order to make a niche for themselves in the American economy. Soon the "Chinese laundry" became a familiar sight in many communities. The laundrymen called their occupation the "Eight Pound Livelihood" because their irons, which were filled with hot coals, weighed eight pounds. Other Chinese immigrants opened hotels, restaurants, dry goods stores, delivery services, and other small businesses that catered both to the ethnic market within the Chinatowns and to the general public as well.

53

This entrepreneurial spirit, in which the immigrant opens his or her own small business, usually staffed by family members, is still an important part of the Chinese experience in America. Since the mid-19th century the Chinese have contributed to major American industries, including mining, farming, and manufacturing, but they have also continued to operate businesses of their own. By the early 1990s, there were about 65 Chinese-owned businesses for every 1,000 Chinese in the United States.

In the early decades, Chinatowns were essentially bachelor societies. Many immigrants could not afford to bring their wives and families with them. In addition, Chinese custom did not approve of women leaving the home, and many Chinese men considered the medical examinations and other immigration procedures to be humiliating for their wives. Therefore, even merchants who could afford to send to China for their entire families were reluctant to do so. After the 1888

◻ *Many Chinese immigrants claimed citizenship after the earthquake that rocked San Francisco and destroyed most of the city's records.*

Scott Act, the immigrants were unable to return to China to marry and bring their new wives to China. Unions between Chinese men and non-Chinese women were discouraged by laws against interracial marriage—but the ratio of Chinese men to Chinese women in America was about 19 to 1. Because relatively few Chinese women immigrated to the United States in these years, an illegal slave trade developed to import them, usually for sale to brothels.

Paper Sons

Many Chinese managed to circumvent immigration restrictions. Some became American citizens before the law prohibited Chinese naturalization. After the San Francisco earthquake and fires destroyed most records in 1906, many residents of San Francisco claimed to have been born in America. And because immigration legislation permitted foreign-born children of citizens to immigrate, many young Chinese purchased falsified documents claiming kinship to American citizens. These new immigrants were called "paper sons."

These "relatives" found the immigration process tedious and often humiliating. They were detained in overcrowded holding centers for days, weeks, and sometimes months before being questioned by immigration inspectors. At first, many were detained in a shed at the Pacific Mail Steamship Company Wharf on San Francisco's waterfront. As the paper sons slowly increased the number of Chinese immigrants after the earthquake, officials transferred their processing center to Angel Island in the San Francisco Bay.

Processing activities on Angel Island began with physical examinations. Chinese women felt humiliated when they had to remove their clothing for the male American doctors. After the physical examination, the immigrants were sent to primitive temporary living quarters while they waited to be interrogated. Men and women, including husbands and wives, were separated until the interrogations were completed.

Aware of the paper son ploy, officials intensified their interrogations. They asked detailed questions, such as "How many steps are there from your house to the village well?" and "What is your bedroom floor made of?" After the immigrant was interrogated, officials contacted his purported American relatives to verify the answers. If the answers didn't match, the immigrant was sent back to China.

Many of the paper sons who had claimed U.S. citizenship used their new status to bring wives from China; because the men were citizens, not merely resident aliens, their wives were allowed to enter the country to join them. Each year from 1910 to 1924, more than 1,000 Chinese

☐ *Many district associations erected altars in their headquarters.*

women came to America this way. The arrival of these women changed the nature of the Chinese community in America. Marriage and family life were woven into the fabric of the Chinatowns, and the ranks of the second-generation Chinese Americans swelled. In 1924, however, the flow of newcomers from China was stopped by a new federal law that banned *all* immigration from Asia. "We were beginning to re-populate a little now," one Chinese man said, "so they passed this law to make us die out altogether."

But the Chinese community in America did not die out, although it was reduced in size. New immigrants could not enter, and those

■ *This funeral procession was probably arranged by a clan association.*

already in the country felt helpless and afraid. Unless they had been born in the United States, they could not become U.S. citizens, and they risked being deported, or sent out of the country, if they were found to have entered illegally. Their fears were heightened in the 1950s by the federal government's Confession Program, which urged paper sons who had falsely claimed citizenship to come forward and confess. Although those who confessed were promised fair treatment, they sometimes found themselves facing legal charges or even threats of deportation. The suspicion and mistrust of that era still haunt Chinese-American communities today. Mistrust of the law and the government may help explain the reluctance of both old and young Chinese immigrants to get involved in politics or complain about injustices—they fear that they will be labeled troublemakers and will ruin their families' and friends' chances to immigrate in the future.

58

Chinese-American Associations

The Chinese in the United States adapted some Chinese customs to American life. For example, in China, entire village populations were usually related to one another and shared the same family name. So, in America, men with the same family name formed clan associations based on real or assumed kinship. The clan associations became surrogate families, providing food, housing, and job information to new arrivals. Their headquarters were places to exchange news and gossip, and even to eat and sleep.

As the number of immigrants and American-born Chinese increased, the clan associations gave way to larger district associations. Members of these associations all came from the same region in China. The district associations were powerful organizations. They collected dues from members, ensured that the immigrants who planned to return to China had paid all their debts, and represented the interests of the Chinese community in the courts and legislatures. In the 1880s the leaders of six district associations formed the Chinese Consolidated Benevolent Association, or Chinese Six Companies, a national organization that continued to play a significant role in Chinese-American affairs until the 1950s.

A third type of Chinese organization was the tong, a secret society that in China was often involved in political dissidence or criminal activity. Tongs were formed in the United States as early as the 1850s;

Missionaries tried to convert the Chinese by teaching them English.

they continue to flourish in New York's Chinatown and other parts of the country today. Some tongs are criminal gangs linked to illegal activities, but tongs have also served as fraternal organizations for both Chinese immigrants and Chinese Americans. The guild is another important Chinese-American institution: since their early days in the

 *Chinese Americans kept their culture and traditions alive.*

United States, Chinese businesspeople, laborers, and artisans have formed their own professional and craft guilds, through which members help one another with jobs, savings and loans plans, and scholarships. The Chinese in America have a long tradition of helping one another through private ethnic groups such as the associations and

■ *A Chinatown musician in the late 19th century. As Chinatowns became tourist attractions, especially in New York City and San Francisco, residents often donned traditional Chinese clothing or assumed picturesque poses to create an exotic image for the non-Chinese visitors.*

guilds, and the notion of self-help is still very much alive in Chinese America. Successful Chinese immigrants and Chinese Americans show their commitment to the ethnic community by donating large sums to neighborhood centers in Chinatowns, societies that preserve traditional Chinese arts and crafts, scholarship funds for Chinese-American students, and religious organizations.

Christian Missionaries

Christian missionaries had gone to China at the turn of the century in an organized effort to convert the Chinese people, and their fund-raising efforts had educated many Americans about the plight of famine-stricken China. In the United States, missionaries helped the Chinese immigrants adapt to American life. One of these missionaries was Reverend William Speer, a Presbyterian physician who opened a San Francisco mission in 1852. Because many Chinese immigrants needed medical treatment after their arduous journey, he also opened a dispensary. In 1853, he began worship services in Chinese and English and opened a Sunday school. He also opened an evening school to teach English and other subjects. Soon, other churches instituted similar programs to teach the Chinese English so that they could understand the gospel.

The missionaries also helped introduce Chinese-language newspapers, believing they would be useful tools for spreading the gospel. The first Chinese-American daily newspaper, the *Chung Sai Yat Po*, was founded by a Christian convert.

After 50 years of work in San Francisco, the Presbyterian missions had baptized only 360 converts, but they had done much to provide needed support services. For many years, the missions and schools were the only American institutions geared to meet the needs of the Chinese Americans. The missionaries opened homes, such as the Ming Quong Girls' Home in Oakland, California, that provided temporary housing for homeless Chinese girls—usually runaways from the brothels.

The churches even provided for the recreational needs of the few children in the Chinese-American community, founding organizations such as the Young Men's Christian Association (YMCA) and the Young Women's Christian Association (YWCA). Although the organizations provided religious as well as social programs, most Chinese-American youths absorbed the American middle-class val-

■ *Mao proclaimed himself leader of the People's Republic of China.*

ues—but not necessarily the religion. Today about 20 percent of the Chinese-American population is Christian.

Another important legacy of the Christian missionaries in China was the goodwill they generated among Americans toward the Chinese people. Writer Pearl S. Buck, the daughter of Presbyterian missionaries, grew up in China and lived there with her first husband, also a missionary. Her books about China and its people—notably *The Good Earth* (1931) and *The House of Earth* (1935)—were enormously popu-

64

lar in the United States and created an audience that was sympathetic to the struggles and sufferings of the Chinese peasant class.

The Birth of Modern China

Political events in China throughout the 20th century have affected both the emigration of the Chinese and the status of Chinese people abroad. China entered an era of sweeping change in the early years of the century, when nationalism—the belief that China should become an independent, modern republic—gained strength. Nationalist forces

Street orators informed crowds about recent events in the homeland.

under the leadership of a progressive, charismatic physician named Sun Yat-sen deposed the Qing dynasty in 1912 and declared China a republic. In the decades that followed, however, China was torn by conflict among regional warlords, the nationalists (led by Sun's successor, Chiang Kai-shek), and the Chinese Communists. In the late 1930s, China was invaded by Japan, and the nationalists and Communists joined forces against this common enemy. During World War II (1939–45), China was an ally of the United States in the fight against Japan. After the war, the Chinese nationalists and communists returned to fighting each other, but this internal struggle ended in 1949, when the Chinese Communist party, led by Mao Zedong, founded the People's Republic of China, a Communist state. The nationalists fled to the offshore island of Taiwan, where they set up a rival government. Mainland China remains a Communist nation in the 1990s.

All of these events touched the lives of the Chinese in America. The immigrants closely followed news of developments in the homeland. There was some support for the communist movement, especially among the Chinese students in the United States. The majority of the Chinese Americans have traditionally been conservative in their political and economic thinking, however, and they overwhelmingly supported the nationalists. Organizations such as the Chinese

Sun Yat-sen led the movement to rid China of foreign intervention.

66

Consolidated Benevolent Association sponsored patriotic rallies in Chinatowns, at which funds were raised to help support the nationalist cause in China. Chiang and the Chinese nationalists also received military and financial aid from the U.S. government, which hoped that the nationalists would keep communism from taking hold in China. When the communists came to power, the U.S. government ended diplomatic relations with mainland China.

World War II improved the status of the Chinese in America. More than 8,000 Chinese-Americans served in the U.S. armed forces. Many served with great distinction. After the war, a number of these ex-soldiers used the G.I. Bill to pay for college educations. The war taught Americans to view the Chinese as allies and friends. In 1943, in the middle of the war, Congress passed a law that permitted immigration from China for the first time in nearly 20 years and also allowed Chinese immigrants in the United States to apply for citizenship. Although the new law limited Chinese immigration to just 105 people each year, several large exceptions were made: more than 6,000 Chinese women entered the country as "war brides," the wives of U.S. servicemen, and several thousand Chinese students were admitted to American colleges after the war.

A New Era in Immigration

In 1965, Congress passed a new federal immigration law designed to eliminate racial or ethnic discrimination in the nation's immigration policy. Immigrants from all Asian countries were once again allowed to enter the United States. China's annual immigration quota was raised from 105 to 20,000. This figure did not include family members of Chinese already living in America, who were free to enter. The 1965 law opened the way for a massive second wave of Chinese immigration that is still continuing today. From 1965 to 1985, four times as many Asians came to America as during the whole previous century, and more than one-quarter of them were Chinese. The Chinese population in the United States grew from 237,000 people in 1960 to 812,000 in 1980 to 1.6 million in 1990. These recent newcomers from China are called the San Yi Man ("new immigrants"), and they have brought new life and energy to Chinese America.

In
PRAISE OF
THE GODS

The Chinese who came to America brought the values and beliefs of their philosophers, religious leaders, and gods. The festivals celebrating these values are based on ancient beliefs that the gods watched over everyone, helping the good and punishing the bad. The Chinese New Year's celebration is an example of such a festival. Before it begins, houses are thoroughly cleaned. Cleaning is forbidden during the festival for fear it will remove the good luck that has just arrived. Red paper, which denotes good luck, is placed throughout the house.

During the festival, Chinatown parades feature a long line of people in a paper dragon costume. The dragon winds through the streets chasing away evil spirits. Shopkeepers hang offerings—usually money—wrapped in red paper above their doors for the dragon to devour.

Such celebrations developed from the ancient Chinese religious and philosophic beliefs of Bud-

69

dhism, Confucianism, Taoism, and ancestor worship. The oldest belief is ancestor worship, evidence of which appears in the intricate bronze work adorning the tombs and burial sites of the 13th century B.C. This traditional reverence toward ancestors takes a variety of forms today. Some households display a plaque or tablet inscribed with ancestors' names. One tradition requires that the names be read while bowing to tablets dedicated to the ancestors' memory. Even many who do not believe that the spirits of their dead ancestors have the power to affect their lives follow this tradition out of respect for the family.

Ancestor worship also includes the practice of visiting ancestral graves during Ching Ming in spring and Chung Yeung in autumn. The ritual includes bringing gifts of food, cleaning the graves, and paying homage to the spirits of the dead ancestors. During the seventh lunar month, people offer food and spirit money to the dead who have no family to perform this ritual.

Another Chinese spiritual belief is *feng-shui*. Practitioners of feng-shui attempt to divine the balance of natural and supernatural forces to determine, for example, the most favorable placement of objects. To this day, believers in feng-shui call for expert advice before build-

Rituals of ancestor worship guide several Chinese celebrations that entail family visits to the burial sites of the deceased.

 *Ancestral graves dot the Chinese landscape.*

ing a house, arranging furniture, or finding a suitable gravesite. They also take feng-shui principles into account in the selection of lucky days for births, marriages, and other special occasions.

Confucianism

While ancestor worship and feng-shui dealt with supernatural forces, the teachings of Confucius (551-479 B.C.) gave the Chinese people a code of behavior based on morality and virtue. Confucianism was applied to both public and private life. This philosophy taught that all men are born good and that anyone can achieve perfection if he follows his own sense of morality. The Confucian concepts of balance and order continued to be developed and refined after Confucius's death until they defined much of Chinese life.

71

Taoism

Taoism has also influenced Chinese philosophy, art, and life. It developed from the philosophy of a contemporary of Confucius, Lao Tze. Perhaps its best-known contribution to Chinese life is the concept of *yin* and *yang*—the balancing forces of the universe, such as light and dark, male and female, and heaven and earth. Taoism offered a mystical counterpoint to Confucianism's hard line of social responsibility. It focused on the transcendental worlds of the spirit and the beauty of nature. Eventually, some Chinese embraced Taoism as the secret of eternal life, and a popular cult religion evolved that espoused superstition and demon lore. For example, many Chinese Americans still practice the ritual of smearing honey on a paper image of the Stove God and burning it on New Year's Eve so that the god will speak sweetly about what he has observed from his place on the kitchen wall. Taoism eventually lost credibility among most Chinese intellectuals, but some of its original elements were absorbed into Confucianism and Chinese Buddhism.

Buddhism

As the first religion to speak of an afterlife, Buddhism had a great impact on China. It was based on the teachings of the Indian philos-

■ *This 17th-century ceramic statue honors the Taoist god of war, Kuan-ti.*

▟

■ *This gilt and bronze Buddhist shrine sets a contemplative tone.*

opher Buddha (563-483 B.C.). Devotional Buddhism emphasized contemplation, adoration, and good works, for example, erecting temples. The heaven, or Nirvana, that Buddha sought was a state of mind with no conscious thought, memory, wish, or desire. The pagodas that Buddhists built represented the earth near the ground and then the world above, as they tapered into the infinite.

The Chinese who came to America expressed these ancient philosophies in many ways. Based on the principles of feng-shui, they built temples ranging from the elaborate to the very plain. They followed the practices of ancestor worship through the Chinese family associations, which often reserved the top floors of their meeting places as temples. Because many of these associations developed from clans, the assembly room often held a tablet or portrait of the clan leader. Chinese-American religious practices still combine the reverence of ancestor worship with the excitement of the Chinese New Year, when dragons chase away bad luck.

73

TIMOTHY DALY · RAYMOND C DAVIS · RAYMON
EARL W JENNINGS · AUGUST D JOHNSON · PAUL
CASIMIR NIESPODZIANY · WILLIAM R PHILLIPS · S
WENDELL SPENCER · JERRY L SPICER · ALVIN G TEN
MORTON E TOWNES Jr · ROBERT D WARE · DAN T
SALVATORE CAMMARATA · ALLAN P COLLAMORE
CHARLES S HYMERS · KENT L JOHNSTONE · GARY
WILLIAM L LOWMAN · THOMAS R MARK · JOSEPH
FRANK M PIPKIN · RUSSELL A POOR + ROBERT L SH
· FRANKLIN B WILLIAMS · JOHN STORELLI · DONALL
WOODROW H WILBURN + ROBERT F STARBUCK ·
JAMES E BOSTOCK · JOSEPH M BRADY · ULYSSES C
ROBERT R ECKER · ROBERT J ELGAARD · JAMES R PA
MELVIN G MOFFETT · JIMMY E MUMFORD · JAMES
DAVID E PRICE Jr · KENNETH D ROBERTS · JAMES H
EVERETT ARMSTRONG · SAMUEL W ARRINGTON Jr
ROGER V P BURKE · JIMMY LEE BUSSEY · GEORGE J
RAYMOND M DARRIGAN · WILLIAM ROBERTS · PAT
WILLIAM E GRAY · DONALD J HALL · LUCIUS L HEIS
· JAMES A LASCHE · JAMES O MILLER · MERRHAGE M
MICHAEL C NEWMAN · THOMAS M NOWACK · WI

14 E

6 Chinese-American Achievements

The modern-day achievements of the Chinese in America permeate the fabric of American life, and several have had international ramifications. Dr. Chen Ning Yang (b. 1922) and Dr. Tsung-Dao Lee (b. 1926) won the Nobel Prize for physics in 1957 for their investigation of parity laws, especially with regard to elementary particles. So important was their work that the *New York Times* compared their accomplishment to the discovery that the earth was round.

Dr. Chien-shuing Wu (b. 1912), a Columbia University physics professor who conducted experiments to prove Dr. Yang's and Dr. Lee's theory, has won many awards, including the 1962 Woman of the Year Award from the Association of American University Women and the Scientist of the Year for Industrial Research Award in 1974. In 1976,

75

the Nobel Prize for physics was awarded to Dr. Samuel C.C. Ting (b. 1936) for his discovery of a new subatomic particle.

Entrepreneur and electronics engineer An Wang, who was born in Shanghai in 1920, left China after World War II to study Western technology in the United States. Shortly thereafter, he became a major contributor to that technology. He received a Ph.D. in physics from Harvard University. Later, he invented the magnetic-core computer memory and sold the invention to IBM. In 1951, Wang used the profits from this sale to finance his own business. Today, Wang Laboratories is a frontrunner in America's highly competitive computer industry, and in 1986 *Forbes* magazine listed Wang as one of the wealthiest people in America. He was honored by President Ronald Reagan with the Medal of Liberty—an award to honor naturalized citizens who have made significant contributions to society—during the July 4, 1986, celebration of the 100th anniversary of the Statue of Liberty.

Artists and Architects

World-renowned cellist Yo-Yo Ma was born in Paris of Chinese parents in 1955. He began playing the cello at age four, gave his first recital at age six, and entered the Juilliard School of Music in 1962, at age seven, where he studied under the legendary Leonard Rose. During the course of his career, Ma has appeared with every major European or American orchestra. In 1978, he was awarded the prestigious Avery Fisher prize.

Chinese-American Maya Lin (b. 1959) won the national design competition for the Vietnam Veterans Memorial (pictured on page 74) in Washington, D.C., in 1981. The daughter of Taiwanese immigrants who settled in Ohio, she had viewed herself as just another American student until criticism of her design and heated opposition to the memorial changed her life and her attitudes. Some believed the criticism stemmed from prejudice toward her as a person of Chinese

 *An Wang's electronics laboratory was originally a one-man shop.*

descent. The incident forced her to question equality in American society and her place in that society:

> The competition was anonymous. No names were allowed on any of the boards. It has always been a question in my mind as to what would've happened if names had been al-

lowed. . . . I hope sometime that people's names can be left on and it won't make a difference. Until that time, I hope I am an example for people who are young and who have a chance to say something when they should.

Although the American dream has been realized by many Chinese Americans, including Maya Lin, some still feel the sting of bias.

Other artists, sculptors, and architects have also achieved international recognition. Architect I.M. Pei, who was born in China in 1917, arrived in the United States at the age of 17 and earned degrees from Harvard University and the Massachusetts Institute of Technology. His projects include the John F. Kennedy Library in Massachusetts, the east wing of the National Gallery of Art in Washington, D.C., the Overseas-Chinese Banking Corporation Center in Singapore, the East-West Center at the University of Hawaii, and the Fragrant Hill Hotel in Beijing.

Sculptor, painter, and engineer Wen-Ying Tsai was born in Xiamen, China, in 1928 and immigrated to America in 1950. He has exhibited his work all over the world and is represented in major international exhibitions and permanent collections at museums such as the Whitney Museum of American Art, in New York, and the Tate Gallery, in London. Working primarily with water, fiber optics, fiberglass, and stainless steel, he is the inventor of the computer mural and has created cybernetic (automatically-controlled) water sculptures in Hong Kong and Singapore.

Literature

Chinese-American writers have made significant contributions to the mainstream of American literature. One of the most popular novels of the 1980s was *The Joy Luck Club* (1989), by Amy Tan; the book was made into a critically acclaimed movie. In this and her 1991 novel *The Kitchen God's Wife*, Tan explored the inner lives of Chinese Americans,

☐ *The John F.
Kennedy Library is one
of I.M. Pei's modern
masterpieces.*

their mixed feelings about Chinatown and their ancestral homeland, and the sometimes troubled relationships between traditional parents and their more Americanized children.

Born in Stockton, California, in 1940, Maxine Hong Kingston has written two autobiographical volumes that have received critical and popular acclaim. *Woman Warrior* won the National Book Critics Circle Award for nonfiction in 1976 and was named one of the best books of the year by *Time* magazine and the *New York Times Book Review*. The second volume, *China Men*, won the 1981 American Book Award and was nominated for a Pulitzer Prize.

Lawrence Yep (b. 1948) began writing when a high school teacher promised to give an A grade to any student who published an article in a national magazine. Yep earned that A by writing a science fiction story that he sold for a penny a word. His first book, *Sweetwater*, was also science fiction. His second book, *Dragon Wings*, was inspired by Fung Joe Guey, the pilot who flew the first aircraft on the West Coast in 1909. Yep won two prizes for *Dragon Wings*: the Newberry Honor Book and the Promising Novel of 1975. Since then, he has published 12 other books, ranging from history to science fiction to mystery.

Playwright David Henry Hwang (b. 1957) achieved success with his first play, *FOB* (Fresh-Off-the-Boat), which explores the conflicts and similarities between two Chinese Americans and a Chinese exchange student. Conceived while Hwang was an undergraduate student at Stanford University, *FOB* was awarded the 1980 Dramalogue Playwriting Award and the 1981 Obie Award for best play. Hwang has written several other plays, including *The Dance and The Railroad*, which revolves around the 1867 railroad strike by Chinese workers. This play was broadcast nationally on the Arts Cable Network.

Media

Prejudice and stereotyping have made the pursuit of theater and film careers difficult for Chinese-American actors, but some who work behind the scenes have enjoyed success. For example, Wah Ming Chang, a self-taught sculptor, created puppets, movies, masks, and models and developed many of the monsters seen on television's *Star Trek* and *Outer Limits*. His special effects for *The Time Machine* in 1970 won an Academy Award.

James Wong Howe (1899-1976), who immigrated to America from China in 1904, turned his talents to film after a short stint as a boxer. Howe became one of the top cinematographers in the world. He was nominated for an Oscar 16 times and won twice, for *The Rose Tattoo* in 1955 and *Hud* in 1964.

Another Chinese immigrant, Ming Cho Lee (b. 1930), has been the principal set designer for the New York Shakespeare Festival since 1962. He also has designed sets for shows such as *Mother Courage*, *Gandhi*, and *The Glass Menagerie*. In 1983, Lee won the Tony Award for set design for the Broadway play *K-2*.

Television network newscaster Connie Chung was born Constance Yu-Hwa Chung in Washington, D.C. The youngest of five daughters, Chung was the only child in the family born in America. Intent on a career in biology, she changed her plans after she worked one summer for a congressman. She became fascinated with Capitol Hill reporting and, in her senior year, changed her major to broadcast journalism. Although Chung believes some job opportunities came because she "had the good fortune of being a minority member as well as a woman," she has worked hard to reach her current status. She has held prominent news posts at both NBC and CBS. Chung won an Emmy in 1978 for individual achievement, the Los Angeles Press Club's TV Reporting Award in 1977, and B'nai B'rith's First Amendment Award in 1981.

Law and Politics

Chinese Americans have also made significant contributions in law and politics. William D. Soo Hoo became the first Chinese-American mayor when he was elected by the citizens of Oxnard, California. Harry Low (b. 1931) is a Superior Court judge in San Francisco.

82

March Fong Eu (b. 1927) is California's secretary of state, and Shin Biau Woo was elected Delaware's lieutenant governor in 1984.

Probably the best-known Chinese-American politician is Hiram L. Fong (b. 1907). Born in Honolulu to immigrant parents who worked on the sugar plantations, Fong worked his way through college, finally graduating from Harvard Law School. He was elected to the Hawaii Legislature (1938-1954) and then to the U.S. Senate (1959-1977). His many accomplishments earned him numerous awards, including the Horatio Alger Award in 1970.

Judge Thomas Tang, the son of an immigrant grocer, currently serves as a judge of the Ninth U.S. Circuit Court of Appeals. Contrasting his success with an earlier time when Chinese immigrants could not even be witnesses in courts of law, Tang told interviewers that anything is possible in America. He began, "I am led to ask the question: What is a Chinaman doing here? It has never happened before. Surely," he concluded, "this is the American Dream at work."

7

CHINESE AMERICANS TODAY

After the passage of the 1965 immigration law, Chinese-American immigration boomed in the late 1960s. Between 1960 and 1970, the population of New York's Chinatown alone leaped from 6,000 to 24,000; by 1980, New York City's Chinese population had grown to 140,000. In the 1970s, improved relations between the People's Republic of China and the United States helped spur the immigration surge. After U.S. president Richard Nixon and Chinese premier Chou En-lai established diplomatic relations in 1972, thousands of Chinese Americans petitioned for the emigration of their relatives in China. A significant number of the new immigrants were fleeing from persecution or repression in Communist China. The quest for personal and political freedom remains a powerful factor in emigration from China today.

The number of citizens' groups increased as the population grew.

Like immigrants from other nations, the Chinese come to America seeking a better life for themselves and their children. Free public education in the United States attracts immigrants from Hong Kong, where school is not affordable for most. Hong Kong's overpopulation is another contributing factor. Because it is difficult for citizens of the People's Republic to obtain their government's permission to enter the United States, many travel first to Hong Kong and from there to the United States. Chinese immigrants also emigrate through Taiwan, Southeast Asia, Trinidad, and Jamaica. In addition to immigrants from the People's Republic, many of the Chinese who have come to the United States in recent years were lifelong citizens of Taiwan, Vietnam, or Hong Kong.

Unlike the first wave of immigrants from China, the post-1965 wave has included many women: more than half of all recent Chinese immigrants are women. Most of the earlier immigrants were laborers or rural farmers, but the majority of the new immigrants come from the cities. Among them are many professionals—doctors, lawyers, teachers, engineers, and scientists.

Some of the new immigrants bring with them enough money to buy their own businesses. Others, particularly those who have not yet mastered English and do not possess professional skills, find that their job opportunities in the United States are limited. They find work in low-paying jobs in the Chinatowns—the men in restaurants or shops, the women in clothing factories.

Family and Community

Traditionally, the family is the central institution of Chinese life. Relationships among family members are shaped by Confucian principles: respect for one's parents, one's ancestors, and all elderly people, and unquestioning obedience to one's father and husband. Tradition granted boys more rights and privileges than girls.

Among Chinese Americans today, the family remains extremely important, although many aspects of Chinese family life have become increasingly Americanized. For one thing, Chinese-American families,

Generational differences are bridged through mutual respect.

Intermarriage has become increasingly common among the younger generations of Chinese Americans.

like all American families, have gotten smaller over the years. As Americans of Chinese descent absorb the American concepts of personal freedom and self-fulfillment, family ties weaken to some degree: divorce and single parenthood, once almost unheard-of among the Chinese, are on the rise among Chinese Americans, although as a group the Chinese Americans still have fewer divorces than the general population.

One source of conflict that all immigrant groups have faced is the tension between parents born in the old country, who often insist that their children adhere to traditional customs and values, and children who grow up in America and want to make different choices. In Chinese-American families, fathers who expect total obedience and respect are sometimes confounded by the independent attitudes their Americanized children display. In her 1945 autobiography, *Fifth Chinese Daughter*, American-born Jade Snow Wong described her struggle to win her father's esteem and approval as she asserted her independence as a modern American woman.

Chinese community life was also shaped by Confucian tradition, which placed a high value on work, self-help and self-reliance, thrift, education, and respect for others in the community. The lives of Chinese immigrants and Chinese Americans have reflected these values. For the most part, the Chinese in America are more likely to have sav-

88

ings than to be in debt. It is not uncommon for an entire extended family to work together to save enough money to open a business or to send a young person to a good college. Chinese Americans generally avoid welfare programs; when they need help, they turn to family members, ethnic associations or guilds, and their fellow Chinese.

Chinese Americans place a high value on education. In 1980, 47 percent of Chinese-American men and 33 percent of Chinese-American women between the ages of 25 and 64 had completed four years or more of college, compared with 22 percent of white American men and 14 percent of white American women. The scholastic achievements of Chinese Americans are notable. As a group, Chinese-American students outperform the general student population in science and math, and students of Chinese descent are well represented at the nation's most prestigious colleges and universities. Yet the outstanding achievements of many Chinese-American students have tended to obscure the fact that others, particularly among the recent immigrants with poor English skills, are struggling to do well in school and have the same educational needs and problems as non-Chinese students. Some members of the Chinese-American community are concerned that high scholastic performance by Chinese as well as other Asian students has created a kind of reverse stereotype, an image of Chinese or of Asians in general as a "model minority." Such an image, while less hurtful than older ethnic stereotypes, still fails to do justice to the individuality and diversity of Chinese Americans.

Assimilation

The flow of new immigrants in recent years has meant that the Chinese population in the United States now contains more foreign-born than American-born individuals. Many of the newcomers have settled in the large and booming Chinatowns of New York City, Los Angeles, and San Francisco. Yet most will not remain there. For many Chinese immigrants today, Chinatown is a point of entry, not a lifetime home. The great majority of Chinese immigrants are eager to learn or perfect their English, to get their children enrolled in English classes, to find good jobs, and to move into the mainstream of American society. Today Chinese Americans are more urban than the general U.S. population—96 percent of all Chinese live in urban or suburban settings, compared with 75 percent of the total population. But they are no longer concentrated in Chinatowns; indeed, they live in all parts of major cities and in the suburbs as well. If, as many sociologists claim, the suburb is the symbol of "the American dream," then Monterey Park, California, is a milestone in Chinese-American history. In 1988, more than half of this suburban community's residents were of Chinese descent. Monterey Park had a Chinese mayor, Lilly Chen, and Chinese real-estate developer Fred Hsieh was calling the area "a Chinese Beverly Hills."

Another sign of the degree to which people of Chinese descent are moving into the larger society is intermarriage. In the early years of Chinese immigration, intermarriage between Chinese and whites was rare; in some states, it was illegal. Chinese tradition, too, discouraged relationships with non-Chinese. The laws were repealed long ago, and the tradition is breaking down as the United States moves closer to genuine integration. Today nearly one-quarter of all Chinese men in the United States marry non-Chinese women, and about 12 percent of Chinese women marry non-Chinese men. Chinese Americans are more likely than any other Asian group except Japanese to marry non-Asian spouses.

From Michael Chang in tennis to Connie Chung in television news, people of Chinese descent have become part of the mainstream of American society. Their efforts have helped build America, from the transcontinental railroad to the computer industry to the inner-city grocery store. Their cultural contributions, from Chinese food to the best-selling fiction of Amy Tan, are part of the texture of everyday life in the United States. Like every immigrant group, the Chinese Americans have struck their own ever evolving balance between assimilation and ethnic identity, remaining Chinese while becoming American.

FURTHER READING

Chen, Jack. *The Chinese of America: From the Beginnings to the Present*. New York: Harper & Row, 1981.

Chinn, Thomas W., Lai, H. Mark, and Choy, Philip, eds. *A History of the Chinese in California*. San Francisco: Chinese Historical Society of America, 1969.

Hoobler, Dorothy and Thomas Hoobler. *The Chinese American Family Album*. New York: Oxford University Press, 1994.

Mark, Diane Mei Lin, and Chih, Ginger. *A Place Called Chinese America*. Dubuque, Iowa: Kendall Hunt, 1982.

McCunn, Ruthanne Lum. *Chinese American Portraits: Personal Histories, 1828–1988*. San Francisco: Chronicle Books, 1988.

Nee, Victor, and Nee, Brett de Barry. *Longtime Californ': A Documentary Study of an American Chinatown*. Boston: Houghton Mifflin Co., 1974.

Takaki, Ronald. *Ethnic Islands: The Emergence of Urban Chinese America*. New York: Chelsea House, 1994.
————. *Journey to Gold Mountain: The Chinese in 19th-Century America*. New York: Chelsea House, 1994.

Wilson, John. *Chinese Americans*. Vero Beach, Fla.: Rourke Corporation, 1991.

Yung, Judy. *The Chinese Women of America*. Seattle: University of Washington Press, 1986.

Index

Picture credits

The Bettmann Archive: p. 54; California State Library Picture Collection: pp. 12–13, 15, 28–29, 32, 52–53, 58, 60–61, 62, 65, 70; Bill Chen: p. 86; Tom Davies: p. 48 (top and center); *Frank Leslie's Illustrated Newspaper*: p. 37; ICM Artists, Ltd.: p. 78; John F. Kennedy Library: p. 80; Library of Congress: pp. 14, 31, 38–39, 59, 71; *London Illustrated News*: p. 22; NBC, Inc.: p. 82; New York Convention and Visitors Bureau: pp. 16–17, 45, 84–85; New York Public Library Picture Collection: pp. 23, 30, 34, 42, 43, 44, 47 (bottom), 48 (bottom), 49, 50, 56–57, 64, 72, 73, 87; John Schultz, PAR/NYC: pp. 46, 47 (top); Southern Pacific Railroad: p. 35; John L. Stoddard's Lecture Series courtesy of PAR/NYC: pp. 18–19, 20, 21; UPI/Bettmann Newsphotos: pp. 66, 68–69, 74–75; Wang Laboratories: p. 77. Picture research: PAR/NYC.
Cover photos courtesy of California State Library, Sacramento, California, and New York Convention and Visitors Bureau.

WILLIAM DALEY is a freelance writer who has written books and articles on a wide range of subjects, from European literary history to contemporary Asian cuisine. He lives in New York City.

SANDRA STOTSKY is director of the Institute on Writing, Reading, and Civic Education at the Harvard Graduate School of Education as well as a research associate there. She is also editor of *Research in the Teaching of English,* a journal sponsored by the National Council of Teachers of English.

Dr. Stotsky holds a bachelor of arts degree with distinction from the University of Michigan and a doctorate in education from the Harvard Graduate School of Education. She has taught on the elementary and high school levels and at Northeastern University, Curry College, and Harvard. Her work in education has ranged from serving on academic advisory boards to developing elementary and secondary curricula as a consultant to the Polish Ministry of Education. She has written numerous scholarly articles, curricular materials, encyclopedia entries, and reviews and is the author or co-author of three books on education.

REBECCA STEFOFF is a writer and editor who has published more than 50 nonfiction books for young adults. Many of her books deal with geography, environmental issues, and exploration, including the three-volume set *Extraordinary Explorers*. She has worked with Ronald Takaki in adapting *Strangers from a Distant Shore* into a 15-volume Chelsea House series, the ASIAN AMERICAN EXPERIENCE. Stefoff studied English at the University of Pennsylvania, where she taught for three years. She lives in Portland, Oregon.

REED UEDA is associate professor of history at Tufts University. He graduated summa cum laude with a bachelor of arts degree from UCLA, received master of arts degrees from both the University of Chicago and Harvard University, and received a doctorate in history from Harvard.

Dr. Ueda was research editor of the *Harvard Encyclopedia of American Ethnic Groups* and has served on the board of editors for *American Quarterly, Harvard Educational Review, Journal of Interdisciplinary History,* and *University of Chicago School Review.* He is the author of several books on ethnic studies, including *Postwar Immigrant America: A Social History, Ethnic Groups in History Textbooks,* and *Immigration.*

DANIEL PATRICK MOYNIHAN is the senior United States senator from New York. He is also the only person in American history to serve in the cabinets or subcabinets of four successive presidents–Kennedy, Johnson, Nixon, and Ford. Formerly a professor of government at Harvard University, he has written and edited many books, including *Beyond the Melting Pot, Ethnicity: Theory and Experience* (both with Nathan Glazer), *Loyalties,* and *Family and Nation.*